The Greatest Cottage I Ever Lived In

Written by
Dennis Meadows

Illustrated by
Laura Byler

Copyright @2020 by Dennis Meadows

All rights reserved. No part of this book may be reproduced in any form or by any electronic or mechanical means, including information storage and retrieval systems, without permission in writing from the publisher, except by reviewers, who may quote brief passages in a review.

This publication contains the opinions and ideas of its author. It is intended to provide helpful and informative material on the subjects addressed in the publication. The author and publisher specifically disclaim all responsibility for any liability, loss or risk, personal or otherwise, which is incurred as a consequence, directly or indirectly, of the use and application of any of the contents of this book.

WORKBOOK PRESS LLC
187 E Warm Springs Rd,
Suite B285, Las Vegas, NV 89119, USA

Website:	https://workbookpress.com/
Hotline:	1-888-818-4856
Email:	admin@workbookpress.com

Ordering Information:
Quantity sales. Special discounts are available on quantity purchases by corporations, associations, and others.
For details, contact the publisher at the address above.

ISBN-13:   978-1-954753-24-2 (Paperback Version)
               978-1-953839-36-7 (Digital Version)

REV. DATE: 04/11/2020

This little story is to help children and parents alike.

I want to honor my parents who tried to raise me right.

I want to start with Ephesians 6:1-3.

Children, obey your parents in the Lord: for this is right.

Honour thy father and mother;

which is the first commandment with promise;

that it may be well with thee,

and thou mayest live long on the earth.

My story starts when I was about six years old. It was about spring, I guess, and I hadn't started school yet. We moved to the country and rented a little cottage. It was kind of run-down but at least it was a roof over our heads. The town we lived near was called Fredericktown.

The cottage was on a small farm. It had a long gravel lane. At the end of the lane was a stop sign which my dad didn't always stop at like he was supposed to. Then, one day, a highway patrol man was waiting for him, but he just gave my dad a warning. My dad stopped at the sign after that.

Living in the country was like heaven on earth to me. We had a barn and cattle and we had a few chickens and a goose. We ate the eggs from the chickens and the big eggs from the goose too.

I remember one day, one of our red hens came out of the barn with twelve baby chicks behind her. It was a very cute sight to behold. My grandma was there that day and we watched them for a time. It reminds me of the words Jesus spoke about Israel, which could be used for the children of today. *How often have I desired to gather your children together as a hen gathers her brood under her wings. He also said in the Psalms Come, O children, listen to me; I will teach you the fear of the Lord.*

We hadn't been at our cottage long when we got a pony. It was given to us by the owners who couldn't handle it. Well, we couldn't either. My oldest brother Tim was about thirteen at the time and my dad let him ride it in the field. It seemed it went about fifty miles an hour. My dad finally got it stopped and no one else rode it. My dad was big into hunting and fishing. He had a very good bird dog that he used to go hunting with. He would use it to get pheasants, and almost always brought two or more home.

It was at this country cottage that we would go into the woods and pick wild mushrooms. Many times we would come back with three or four paper bags full. We would usually do this on Saturdays in April and my mom would fry the mushrooms we found in butter. They were delicious. We would have them for meals many times.

We would also go and pick blackberries; sometimes three five-gallon buckets at a time. My grandma would come and pick too and take five gallons of berries with her when she left. One time one of my aunts came over to pick berries and I jumped the fence where the bull and cows were. The bull chased me back on my side. I barely made it by rolling under the barbed wire. His horns almost got me and I got cut by the barbed wire. We didn't pick berries that day. It was one day

I really should have listened to my mom.

On Fridays, when my dad got paid, he would always bring home a tiny bag of candy or a half a gallon of ice cream. We all would be at the door waiting for him with big smiles on our faces. Those were the good old days.

As the summer got warmer we would go swimming in a creek that was down the lane. It had a deep spot about twelve feet deep and was maybe fifteen feet long by twelve or fifteen feet wide. We would go swimming almost every Saturday in the summer even though leeches would get on us. My dad saved me many times in that swimming hole.

When I was seven, I started first grade. I remember the first day of school. The bus came and I told the driver I wasn't going, and I didn't go that day. When my dad came home I found out what Proverbs 29:15 and Proverbs 13:24 say. *The rod and reproof give wisdom.* He spanked me and I learned fast. It was a bare spanking and it hurt! The next day I got on the bus. At school I had a hard time for a couple of weeks until I got used to it.

On my ninth birthday, my grandma came over and gave me nine silver dollars, real silver. I remember hiding them in the kitchen but when we moved, we couldn't find them. Years later when the house was torn down, someone got a bonus!

It was about June or July when it was time to bale the hay for about twenty-six head of cattle. I remember I was about nine years old. They had an old tractor and when it was started I asked my dad if I could drive it and he said yes. I jumped on it, and before long I was a young farmer. It was fun. My uncle came to help and we baled straw all day long. We also hired some country boys to help us.

One time around Christmas, a man dressed as Santa came to our home. This man worked at the same place as my dad. My grandma would always bring us oranges, bananas, and English walnuts for Christmas. We only got one or maybe two presents. I got a little toy truck once. I thought I was going to be a truck driver. I played with that truck in the dirt every day. My mom wondered how I got so dirty.

One time someone came to our house and told me Jesus was a carpenter. It was after that I went out into the woods and swung on the vines. It was nice and quiet out there in the country. I talked with God and I told God I wanted to be a carpenter. It was a good long talk and he talked back through the Holy Spirit. I guess I talked for over two hours because my mom was calling for me when I came home.

Ten Years Later

Even with all the fond memories I had of our little country cottage, it was not the greatest cottage. The greatest cottage was my uncle and aunt's house in Sulphur, Louisiana. I was staying with them for a few days. I guess I was running from God. My uncle had a few cattle in the field. In the field was also an old hog pen.

One morning, I went out and sat on the fence of that old hog pen. It was just for a few minutes and the Holy Spirit came upon me greatly and I could hear the voice of Jesus. The words were from John 14:6. *I am the way, the truth, and the life. No man cometh to the Father but by me.* It was there that I bowed my head and I asked Christ into my heart. A great burden left and I was truly saved. To me, the greatest cottage was where I was saved.

www.ingramcontent.com/pod-product-compliance
Lightning Source LLC
Chambersburg PA
CBHW082041080526
44578CB00009B/798